ALL KINDS OF NOSES

Sara Swan Miller

mc **Marshall Cavendish**
Benchmark
New York

Marshall Cavendish Benchmark
99 White Plains Road
Tarrytown, New York 10591-9001
www.marshallcavendish.us

Editor: Doug Sanders
Publisher: Michelle Bisson
Art Director: Anahid Hamparian
Series Designer: Alex Ferrari

Library of Congress Cataloging-in-Publication Data

Miller, Sara Swan.
  Noses / by Sara Swan Miller.
     p. cm. — (All kinds of ...)
  Summary: "An exploration of animal noses, their various shapes and
functions"—Provided by publisher.
  Includes bibliographical references (p. 47) and index.
  ISBN-13: 978-0-7614-2522-9
  1. Nose—Juvenile literature. I. Title. II. Series.

  QL947.M645 2007
  599.14'4—dc22

                                   2006019715

Photo research by Anne Burns Images
Cover photo: Corbis/Kevin Schafer

The photographs in this book are used by permission and through the courtesy of: *Peter Arnold Inc.*: Fritz Polking, 1; Martin Harvey, 4; Rudolf Schnorrenberg, 14; Bruce Lichtenberger, 18; Norbert Wu, 20; Klein, 40. *Corbis:* Royalty Free, 7; Richard Cummins, 8; Micro Discovery, 10; Ron Boardman/Frank Lane Picture Agency, 11; Robert Pickett, 13; DK Limited, 16; Stephen Frink, 21; Bruce Robison, 22; Martin Harvey, 24, 30; Michael & Patricia Fogden, 27; Robert Holmes, 29; Joe McDonald, 31, 34; Tobias Bernhard/zefa, 32; Natalie Fobes, 36; Adrianna Williams/zefa, 37; Helmut Heintges/zefa, 38; Morton Beebe, 43; Bob Strong/Reuters, 44. *Animals Animals:* OSF/C. Milkins, 12; Marian Bacon, 35; Zigmund Leszczynski, 45.

Printed in Malaysia
1 3 5 6 4 2

CONTENTS

1. BY A NOSE   5

2. CAN A MOTH SMELL?
   DO INSECTS INHALE?   9

3. FISHY NOSES   15

4. WHAT ABOUT AMPHIBIANS
   AND REPTILES?   25

5. BIRD "NOSES"   33

6. MARVELOUS MAMMAL NOSES   39

GLOSSARY   46

FIND OUT MORE   47

INDEX   48

*An elephant's trunk is longer
than any other animal's nose.*

1

BY A NOSE

When you think of animal noses, what do you picture? Maybe you think of the cool, moist nose of a dog. Perhaps you picture a rabbit's twitching nose. Maybe you even think of an elephant's long, dangling trunk.

What about your own nose, sticking out from the front of your face? What would you do without it? You certainly would have trouble breathing. The air you breathe through your nostrils travels down your windpipe to your two lungs. Your lungs are lined with blood vessels that absorb or take in the oxygen in the air and carry it all through your body. Muscles in your chest help you breathe in and out. Usually, you breathe without even thinking about it.

Our noses are also good for something else— smelling. Drifting all around us in the air are tiny bits called *odor particles*. You cannot see them, but you can smell them. You draw in the tiny particles with your nostrils, which are lined with hairs. They keep things such as sand and insects from getting inside your nose. The odor particles pass through a kind of chamber called the *nasal cavity*. Then they move to the *olfactory bulb*, where there are thousands of nerve cells.

HOW'S YOUR SNIFFER?

If you have a good sniffer, you can tell the difference between up to 10,000 smells.

So how do you know certain smells and tell different ones apart? Many scientists think that each smell particle fits into its own nerve cell like a key into a lock. The nerve cells then send messages along your *olfactory nerve* to your brain, where they are decoded. Daffodils? Coffee? Peaches? Or skunk!? Your brain can sort out the different smells immediately.

Humans are able to smell only seven main odors:

Musky—Aftershave or Perfume
Roses—Floral Bouquet
Peppermint—Breath Mints or Mint Gum
Putrid—Rotting Meat
Pungent—Vinegar
Camphoric—Moth Balls
Etheral—Cleaning Fluid

Because people are limited to knowing seven main odors, that may explain why it is hard for us to describe a smell to someone who has not smelled it before. Usually, the best we can do is to compare the smell to something else. We might say something smells like roses, or bubble gum, or soap. But we cannot describe smells as well as we can describe an object we can see.

Our noses do more than help us breathe and smell, they also help us taste. The taste buds on our tongue can only detect five tastes—sweet, sour, salty, bitter, and savory. The aromas drifting from our plate to our nostrils are what tell us whether we are eating an apple or an onion. If you hold your nose, you cannot tell the difference. You may have noticed this when your nose was stuffed up from a bad cold. Your food probably did not seem to have much flavor at all.

Our noses help us taste, whether we want to or not.

Aromas also have a way of bringing up old memories. Maybe you smell new tar on the road and remember a trip to the beach long ago. Or maybe you catch a whiff of perfume that calls up the image of your mother dressed and ready for a party. Even more than a picture, an aroma can bring back past scenes in an instant.

Many animals have noses like ours that they use for both breathing and smelling. But many animals do not. Many don't even have nostrils. How can they breathe and smell? Let's find out while taking a look at all kinds of snouts and noses.

A monarch butterfly can taste and smell with its feet.

CAN A MOTH SMELL? DO INSECTS INHALE?

For most insects, their sense of smell is one of their most important ways of exploring the world around them. It is also key in finding food and mates. Insects' bodies are covered with sensitive hairs, especially on their lower legs and head. These hairs help insects smell and taste. There are more *smell receptors* on their antennas, their mouth-parts, as well as on the *ovipositor,* the organ females use to lay eggs. Bees and butterflies use their sense of smell to find flowers full of nectar. Beetles and flies locate decaying animals with their fine sense of smell.

Cockroaches and ants rely heavily on their sense of smell. Cockroaches live in dark places, and they use

A SMELLY TRAP
Some plants actually use their bad odors to capture flies. These plants smell like rotting flesh, an odor that draws in flies. When one goes inside the plant, it gets trapped there. As it struggles, it picks up pollen on its body. When it is finally free, it may carry the pollen to another plant of the same species and fertilize it.

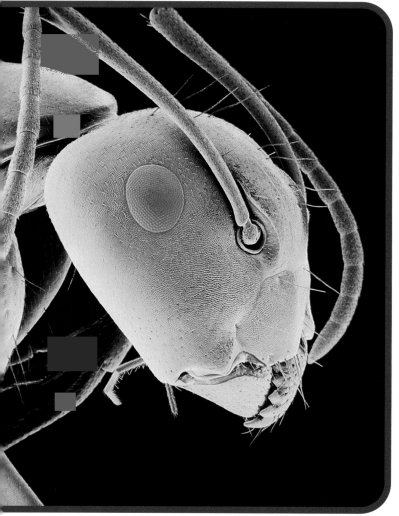

Ant antennas are highly sensitive. They help ants find the scent trails that lead to a food source.

their long antennas to pick up the smell of food. Ants smell mostly with their antennas too. As one travels along in search of food, it leaves behind a scent trail of formic acid. When the ant finds something good to eat, it follows the scent trail back to the nest. Other ants then join together and follow the scent trail to the food source. That way they can bring more food back to the nest. Ants also use their antennas to tell the difference between an ant that is a member of the colony and a stranger that is not. Strangers are killed or driven away.

Some species of insects find their mates by using their excellent sense of smell. Female moths, for example, give off chemical scents called *pheromones*. Each species has its own special pheromones. The males are drawn to the scents and fly off to find the females. The males can smell the pheromones from far away. Emperor moths can track down a female flying about 3 miles (5 kilometers) away. Silkworm moths can detect pheromones up to 7 miles (11 kilometers) away.

How do insects breathe? You have probably guessed that they do not breathe through their noses. Most insects have ten pairs of openings called spiracles along their sides. Air is drawn through the spiracles and into their *tracheas,* which are tubes branching out inside their whole body. Insects can close up their spiracles when they need to, so an insect won't drown even in the heaviest rain.

Insects that live in the water have special problems when it comes to breathing. How do they get enough

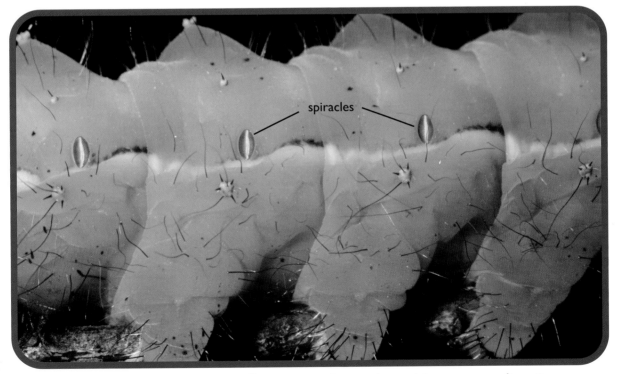

spiracles

Like all insects, this caterpillar's spiracles or breathing organs line its body.

oxygen when they are underwater? Each species has a way of solving the breathing problem. Some insects are like scuba divers. A backswimmer, for instance, collects silvery bubbles of air on the underside of its body. It can stay underwater breathing this air supply for several minutes. A diving beetle breathes air trapped in a chamber under its wings. When it runs out of air, it comes to the surface for more.

A water scorpion uses a different method. It has a long tube at the end of its *abdomen*. When it needs to breathe, it sticks the tube up into the air, like a snorkel. Mosquito *larvae* also have breathing tubes on their abdomens. They hang from the surface, tail up, feeding on algae and bacteria underneath.

A water scorpion stays underwater by sticking its snorkel-like breathing tube above the surface.

Immature aquatic insects, called *naiads*, usually breathe through their gills. Mayfly naiads, for instance, have leaflike gills on the sides of their abdomen. These gills absorb oxygen from the water. Dragonfly naiads have their gills inside their rectal chamber, where they force water in and out. As an extra bonus, a dragonfly naiad can move itself through the water by forcing water out—like a jet rocket taking off.

It is hard to imagine breathing through your tail or through your sides. Being able to smell with your toes is hard to imagine too. And can you imagine being able to smell your friend 7 miles (11 kilometers) away? Insects get along quite well without noses!

A mosquito larva hangs from the water's surface, breathing through its tail.

SMELLY FEET?

Female mosquitoes are drawn to human body odors, especially foot odor. So keep your feet clean!

The nostrils on this long-jawed squirrelfish are just for smelling.

3

FISHY NOSES

Look closely at a fish's snout. Can you see its nostrils? Even though a fish has nostrils, it does not use them to breathe. Instead, it gulps water with its mouth and forces the liquid out through its gill slits. The gills form a curtain that separates the mouth cavity from the gill cavities, so the water must pass through the gills. Fish have the most efficient gills of any water-breathing animal. This is important because water is dense and contains only $\frac{1}{30}$ of the oxygen that air does. Fish must work harder to get the oxygen they need.

A few kinds of fishes can actually breathe air. A lungfish has gills, but it also has one or two *swim bladders* lined with blood vessels. The swim bladders act like lungs, absorbing oxygen from the air the lungfish swallows. As long as it is swimming in freshwater, the lungfish breathes with its gills. But in muddy or stagnant water, it rises to the surface to gulp air.

A mudskipper spends a lot of its time out of water,

GREAT GILLS!

A fish's gills can draw up to 95 percent of the oxygen from the water that passes through them.

15

A mudskipper has no lungs, but it can still breathe out of the water.

skipping through the mud. Yet it has no lungs. Instead, it stores water in spongy sacs found around its gills and in its mouth. When the water gets stale, the mudskipper draws in freshwater from puddles. It can also absorb oxygen through bumps on its skin and tail. Sometimes it also breathes through the wet lining of its mouth. That is why you might see a mudskipper resting on the mudflats with its mouth open.

A clingfish spends a lot of time out of water, but it doesn't have lungs, either. It has a patch of skin on its belly that is full of blood vessels. When the clingfish needs to breathe, it raises the front of its body off the rocks where it is resting and takes in oxygen through its belly patch. Like the mudskipper, a clingfish can also absorb oxygen through the moist lining of its mouth.

A climbing perch can last a long time out of water because it has a special breathing system. At the top of its gill chamber are hollow structures lined with blood vessels. These structures are complex, like a maze or labyrinth, which is why these fish are also known as labyrinth fish. As a climbing perch grows, its breathing organs become ever more complex. Added folds and twists in the organs let the perch get even more oxygen from the air.

When a walking catfish finds its pool is getting stagnant or no longer fresh, it simply leaves and walks to a new body of water. It does not have lungs, but it does have tree-shaped breathing organs on the top of its gill chambers. So if you ever see a fish walking across the road, it might be a walking catfish on moving day.

A fish's nostrils are not any good for breathing, but they are a great aid for smelling. All fish have an excellent sense of smell. They have complex nasal passages, and large parts of the brain are devoted to smelling. Fish nostrils do not lead to the *pharynx,* as ours do. Instead, various fish have different kinds of flow-through systems. Some fish have a flap dividing the nostril into two passages, with an incoming passage and an outgoing one. Some species have a U-shaped tube, lined with tiny hairs that push a current of water through. Still others have a thin membrane that separates the nostril from the mouth cavity. Breathing water through its mouth also forces a stream in and out of its nostrils.

A good sense of smell is important to fish, because they often cannot see well in murky water. They use their sense of smell to alert themselves to possible danger, as well as to find their prey. If a bear is fishing in the water upstream, for example, a fish can smell the bear's chemicals using its skin.

Fish can smell pheromones from other fish as well. When a minnow is wounded, it releases a fear pheromone that tells other minnows, "Swim away!" Pheromones that some deep-sea female fishes give off tell their male mates just where to find them, even in dark or murky water.

Fish can smell grizzly bears when they are upstream. This salmon got caught anyway.

Homing salmon rely on their sense of smell to find their way back to the stream where they hatched years ago. As the newly hatched fry or young swim off to the ocean, the smells along the route are recorded by their brain. On the way back upstream to mate and lay eggs, the odors the salmon recognize along the way guide them. Scientists discovered that if they plugged the nostrils of returning salmon, they could not find their way back home.

BEWARE OF SHARKS!

Sharks have an especially sharp sense of smell. Two-thirds of a shark's brain is dedicated to the sense of smell. Smelling is the best way for a shark to find its prey, and it reacts especially strongly to the scent of blood. A shark can detect a single drop of blood in a million drops of water. It can smell prey up to $1/2$ mile (1 kilometer) away.

Smell, as you know, is closely related to the sense of taste. Fish often have taste buds in places other than their tongues. They have taste buds spread across their face and sometimes along their entire body. Some fishes, including catfishes and goatfishes, have barbels hanging from their chins. They use these whisker-like growths to smell, taste, and probe the bottom for tasty food hidden from sight.

Some fish have unique snouts. A sawfish has a long, flat snout like a blade, with needle-like teeth along its edge. This fish uses its snout to burrow and dig into the muddy bottom in its search for prey. A sawfish will also use its snout as a weapon, slashing among schools or

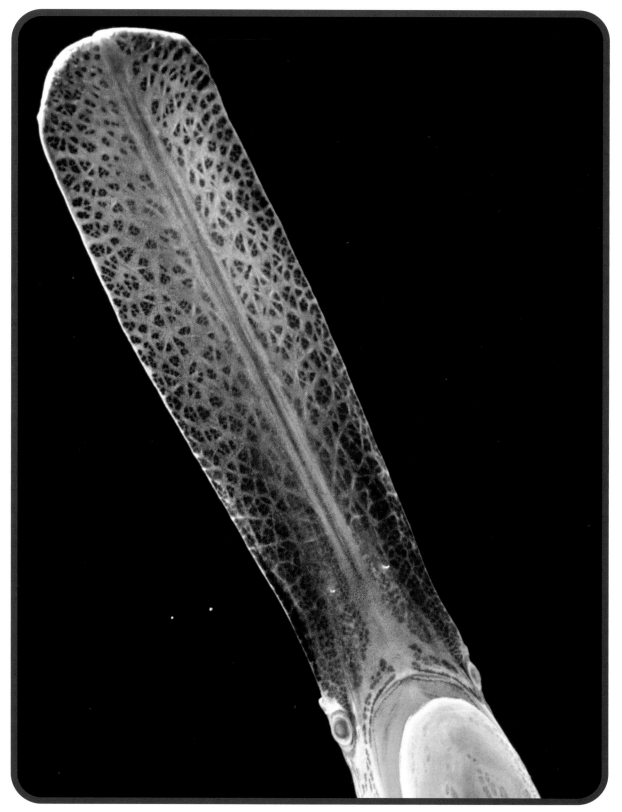

A paddlefish uses its long snout to sense its prey.

groups of small fish to injure them. Then it can gobble up the wounded fish.

Paddlefishes have incredibly long snouts. Some have flat snouts one-third as long as their body. Paddlefishes use their snouts to sense swarms of *plankton*. Then they swim through the swarm, with their jaws wide open, and swallow their prey.

Most fishes with long snouts have nostrils at the base of the snout. But gars have their nostrils at the tip. Gars use their long snouts to snap up fish, crabs, and even birds.

Some moray eels also have unique snouts. One species has large nose tubes sticking out. Another species, the leaf-nosed moray, has leafy flaps all over its snout—the better to smell its prey.

A spotted moray has nose tubes that help it smell prey.

A "fishing frog" is a fish that has developed a good trick for catching prey. On the tip of its snout is a spine covered with flaps of skin. The fishing frog lies in wait on the ocean floor, well hidden in the sand, and wiggles its lure. Bottom-feeding fish think the lure is a possible meal. When a fish comes near the bobbing lure, the fishing frog snaps up its curious prey instead and swallows it down in one gulp.

Female deep-sea anglerfishes also use lures to attract their prey. A Paxton's whipnose angler has a long bony rod on her nose, with a bulb on the end. This part acts

An anglerfish's dangling lure draws in its prey.

like a fishing rod. It extends back past her long body. The males do not have fishing lures, and they have small, weak jaws. They cannot hunt for themselves, but they manage to survive just the

same. They have huge smelling organs that help them find a female in the vast ocean. On their snout and chin they have little hooks. When a male finally finds a female, he latches onto her and waits until she is ready to mate. Sometimes the male's skin fuses with the female's, and he is fed through her blood.

Swordfish and marlins also have unique snouts. Both of them have sword-like blades on their snouts. They use their blades to slash at their prey as they swim by. Then they turn back and gobble up the injured fish.

As these fishes show, noses can be good for more than just smelling.

*A giant bullfrog breathes
mostly through its nostrils.*

WHAT ABOUT AMPHIBIANS AND REPTILES?

How do amphibians breathe? That depends on which ones you are talking about. Amphibian means "double life." Most amphibians spend their larval stage, a time in their early lives, in the water. Their adult lives are then spent on land. That means that the young have a different way of breathing than the adults do.

Most toads, frogs, and salamanders start off as tadpoles living in the water. They gulp water with their mouths and nostrils and force it over their gills. Usually these gills disappear as the larva turns into an adult, but not always. Mudpuppies, for instance, which live mostly in the water as adults, keep their gills their entire lives.

Usually an adult amphibian breathes with its lungs. A frog has nostrils like valves. When it has a mouthful of air, it closes off its nostrils. Then it tightens its throat and drives the air into its lungs.

Frogs, toads, and salamanders have a backup breathing system as well. They actually rarely fill their lungs, but get a lot of oxygen through the lining of their mouths as well as through their moist skin. Watch a frog and you will see it pulsing its throat, moving it in and out. The pulsing creates a flow of water or air over its mouth and throat, which are each lined with blood vessels that easily absorb oxygen.

Some adult amphibians do not have lungs. These include the dusky salamanders, cave salamanders, slimy salamanders, and several others. Most of the lungless salamanders spend their adult lives on land. So how do they breathe? The lining of their mouths is full of blood vessels that absorb oxygen. They also breathe with their skin, which is thin, with many small blood vessels under the surface. As long as a lungless salamander keeps moist, it can absorb oxygen through its skin. But if it dries out, it will suffocate or die from a lack of oxygen.

The hellbender has lungs, but it breathes through its skin. Its skin is baggy and wrinkled, which increases its surface area so it can absorb even more oxygen from the water. Giant salamanders are relatives of the hellbender. They include the large Japanese giant salamanders and the even larger Chinese giant salamanders. They, too, breathe mostly through their baggy skin.

Amphibians have an excellent sense of smell. They have a smelling organ in their noses called a *vomeronasal organ*. It lies in the nasal cavity and allows amphibians to smell and taste at the same time. Nerve fibers from the organ connect

LOTS OF LUNGLESS SALAMANDERS

There are about 250 species of lungless salamanders in the world.

Salamanders can breathe through their wet skin.

with an amphibian's olfactory lobes in the brain, an area that deals with the sense of smell.

Lungless salamanders also have special *nasolabial grooves* on each side of their snout. They are ridges that run from the edge of the upper lip to the nostril. As lungless salamanders crawl along the damp ground, they tap it with their snouts. Fluids they pick up travel along the grooves to the nostrils and from there into the vomeronasal organ. The nasolabial grooves help salamanders find food and recognize one another. A female red-backed salamander uses her nasolabial grooves to smell the droppings of males. If the droppings smell as though a male has been eating well, that sends her a signal that he would be a strong and healthy mate.

Caecilians are little-known amphibians that look like large worms. They live underground or in murky waters, and they cannot see or even hear very well. But they have a fine sense of smell. On each side of their head, between the eye and the nostril, there is an opening. A tentacle sticking out of each hole detects chemicals in the air or water and passes the information back to the Jacobson's organ. When a caecilian is swimming or burrowing, it closes off its nostrils, but it can still smell using its nose tentacles.

Can you guess how reptiles breathe? All of them have nostrils on their snouts, and they all have well-developed lungs. Even reptiles that spend most of their time in the water have to come up to the surface to breathe. That is why large fishing nets used in the ocean can be a terrible problem for sea turtles. They often get caught in the nets and, unable to swim to the surface, they struggle wildly until they drown.

Besides breathing with their lungs, turtles that live in the water can also breathe through their mouth and their *cloaca,* an opening in their tail that gets rid of wastes. The skin in their mouth and cloaca is filled with blood vessels and acts like a simple form of gills. This is important when these turtles hibernate, resting on the sea bottom for months at a time. As long as they are resting, they can get enough oxygen without having to come to the surface. But when a sea turtle is active, it needs to breathe with its lungs to get enough oxygen to fuel its movements.

TOPSIDE NOSTRILS

Alligators' nostrils are on the top of their snouts. So alligators can lie just below the surface of the water and still breathe air.

An alligator can still breathe when it is almost entirely underwater.

Snakes are so long and slender that it is hard to see how they can fit lungs inside their bodies. But they do, of course. Their left lung is much smaller than their right lung, which is long and thin. At the end of this long right lung is a sac where snakes store extra air. When a snake is swallowing large prey, its breathing tube is blocked. It can't inhale, but the stored air in the sac keeps it well supplied while it is busy swallowing.

A good sense of smell is important to all reptiles. For

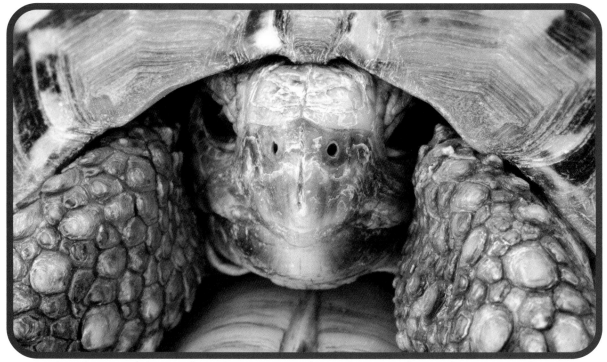

Like the world's turtles, this tortoise breathes air through its nostrils.

many of them, it is their most important sense of all. A tortoise, for instance, does not have very good eyesight or hearing, but it has an excellent sense of smell. It can smell food from far away, although it takes a tortoise a long time to get to it.

Like amphibians, reptiles have two different organs for smelling. They have olfactory organs much like ours, as well as a Jacobson's organ in the roof of their mouth. Have you ever noticed how lizards and snakes are always flicking out their tongues? It may look as though they are trying to scare you, but all they are doing is smelling the air. Their long forked tongues pick up tiny smell particles from the air, then press them onto the Jacobson's organ to sort them out and identify them. These reptiles rely on their excellent sense of smell to track moving prey, find mates, and keep a nose out for predators.

Besides having nostrils, rattlesnakes also have little pits between their eyes and nostrils. The pits may look like extra nostrils, but they are actually heat-sensing organs. Using the pits, rattlesnakes know when a warm-blooded animal is near. Then they can glide silently off in pursuit.

Little pits on this black-tailed rattlesnake's snout allow it to sense the heat given off by its warm-blooded prey.

A kiwi has a strong sense of smell.

5

BIRD "NOSES"

Birds do not have noses, but they do have nostrils. Usually, a bird's nostrils are on top of its bill, near the base. They help a bird breathe.

Birds need a lot of oxygen in order to fly, especially at high altitudes, where the air is thin. A mouse couldn't survive if it found itself on top of Mount Everest, because it wouldn't be able to get enough oxygen. Sparrows, however, would have no trouble at all. A bird's breathing system is much better than a mouse's. When a mouse breathes, it inhales air through its nostrils, and its lungs fill up. When it exhales, its lungs empty. But birds have a different system.

Birds have rather small lungs compared to mice, but they also have air sacs, even inside their hollow bones. When a bird breathes, the air flows through the air sacs first. Then it flows into the tube-like lungs. The air sacs keep a bird's lungs inflated even when it exhales. That means that a bird

KIWI NOSTRILS
Unlike other birds, a kiwi's nostrils are at the tip of its long, slender bill.

can get plenty of oxygen whether it is breathing in or breathing out.

With our lungs, the air moves back along the same path it entered. In a bird, the air follows a circular one-way route through its system. First, air is inhaled through the trachea directly into the rear air sacs. From there it travels into the lungs. From the lungs, the air then moves through the air sacs in the front, where it is exhaled through the trachea. A bird's breathing system takes up 15 to 20 percent of its body. A mouse's respiratory system, like ours, takes up only 5 percent of its body.

How well can birds smell? Most of them do not have

A turkey vulture is known for its sharp sense of smell.

much of a sense of smell—or taste—at all. Birds mostly rely on their eyesight and hearing to find food and mates and to be alert to danger. A sense of smell is just not as key to a bird's survival.

But there are some exceptions. A turkey vulture has an excellent sense of smell. It has one of the largest sets of olfactory organs of any bird. As it soars far above, searching for rotting meat, it can pick up the scent from far off.

Some birds that live near and hunt in the ocean also have a good sense of smell. Shearwaters, albatrosses, and petrels use smell to search out food, mates, and nest sites. Diving petrels have tube-shaped nostrils that open upwards on the top of their bills. The tubes help keep water out of their nostrils when the petrels dive for fish.

THE OTHER VULTURES

Unlike turkey vultures, Old World vultures do not have a strong sense of smell. They rely on their good eyesight instead.

A southern giant petrel uses its good sense of smell to find food far out at sea.

Kiwis—small, flightless birds that live in New Zealand—also have a well-developed sense of smell. Kiwis search for food at night, but, unlike other nocturnal or night-active birds, they do not have very good eyesight. They sniff about on the forest floor searching for insects and other prey. They also probe deep beneath the leaves with their long bills. A kiwi's good sense of smell helps it sniff out danger too. If you scare a kiwi, it will run quickly away. Then, when it thinks it is safe, it stops and sticks its bill in the air, sniffing the air like a dog to be sure it is not being followed.

Scientists have found other birds that may have a good sense of smell. They think that homing pigeons can find their way back to their starting point with the help of "scent maps" they remember from the outbound trip. Scientists have also discovered that if they plug the nostrils of other homing birds,

Crested auklets recognize their mates by the tangerine smell of their feathers.

such as swifts and starlings, the birds have a much harder time getting home.

Scientists have also found out that many different species have a certain odor to their feathers. At courtship time, the odors get much stronger. The feathers of crested auklets smell like tangerines. At courtship time, when the odor is especially strong, the auklets recognize one another by poking their bills into the smelly ruff or neck feathers of their mate. Some birds that mate for life, such as petrels, can recognize their mate by smell even if they have been separated for several weeks. It is their sense of smell that brings them back together.

Chickens avoid the smell of ammonia when they can.

Scientists have even found that some birds turn away from certain smells. Chickens are repelled by the smell of ammonia. That can be hard on chickens on factory farms, where the odor of ammonia can be incredibly strong.

A diving water shrew has an excellent sense of smell, but not when it is underwater.

6

MARVELOUS MAMMAL NOSES

All mammals breathe through the nostrils on our heads. Usually a mammal's nostrils are on its snout. Marine mammals, such as dolphins, whales, and porpoises, are the only exception. Their nostrils, called blowholes, are on the top of their heads. Most of them have just a single blowhole, but baleen whales have two. Marine mammals can stay underwater for a long time holding their breath. But when one needs to breathe, it comes to the surface, blows out the old air, and quickly takes a new lungful of fresh air. Then it dives back down again.

Mammals all have large lungs that fill the chest cavity. A structure under the lungs called a *diaphragm* helps push the air in and out. Mammals are the only animals with a diaphragm. It moves up and down depending on the animal's rate or speed of breathing. Mammals do not all breathe at the same rate. Shrews, for instance, breathe very quickly. They are active creatures and need plenty of oxygen to keep going. A camel, on the other hand, breathes slowly. This is an adaptation to living in the hot, dry desert. When a mammal breathes, it uses up water. A camel breathes only half as fast as a cow and so uses up far less water in the process.

Most mammals have an excellent sense of smell. It is useful, since most mammals are still active at night like their early ancestors. Inside a mammal's nose are special shelf-like structures called *turbinates*. They are bones covered with membranes that create mucus and help trap the smell particles that a mammal breathes in. Most mammals have large olfactory bulbs and lobes in their brains that process smells. Insect-eating mammals have especially large bulbs and lobes and thus a powerful sense of smell. Carnivores or meat eaters and rodents also have large bulbs and lobes and are great smellers. More developed primates such as humans, however, do not have as good a sense of smell.

Porpoises and dolphins have no sense of smell at all. They find their prey using echolocation instead. They bounce sounds off their prey then listen for the echo before closing in.

Most mammals have a much better sense of smell than we do. A cat, for instance, has an olfactory membrane of about 2 square

This husky's nose is one hundred times more sensitive than that of its human friend.

CHAMPION SNIFFERS

A dog's nose is at least a hundred times more sensitive than ours. There may be a million smell cells in each of its nostrils, and the cells are one hundred times larger than ours. A dog's olfactory membrane is even larger than a cat's. It measures up to 23 square inches (150 square centimeters). A dog's nasal cavity is rich with blood vessels and nerve endings that connect to its large olfactory bulbs and lobes. A dog can identify different smells even when they have been covered with skunk spray. People have long used dogs to help track down prey and to find missing people. Now people use dogs to sniff out bombs and drugs in airports and to track down criminals and escaped inmates from prisons. That is one more reason why we call a dog "man's best friend."

inches (14 square centimeters). Our membrane is only ½ square inch (4 square centimeters). So cats can smell odors we do not even notice. Some mammals, including mongooses and lemurs, recognize one another entirely through smell. Many mammals also leave urine behind as scent markers. Wolves, dogs, coyotes, and the little antelopes called dik-diks all leave scent to mark their territory. Another animal can tell by sniffing what was there, what sex it was, and whether it is ready to mate.

Some mammals do not have very good eyesight, but they make up for it with their strong sense of smell. Both grizzly bears and rhinoceroses have poor eyesight, but both of them have great noses. An armadillo also has poor eyesight, but it can sniff out insects 6 inches

(15 centimeters) underground. A koala's tiny eyes are not much help, but it uses its nose to sniff out just the right type of eucalyptus leaves and to find out which leaves can be eaten and which are poisonous.

Like most reptiles and amphibians, most mammals have vomeronasal organs inside their noses. Some mammals, such as horses, deer, and wolves, rely heavily on messages from these organs. When a male deer sniffs a female, he makes a face by curling his upper lip and lifting his head. This gets his vomeronasal organs working so that he can detect scent the female gives off and tell if she is ready to mate or not.

Some mammals have extra-long noses. When you picture long noses, you probably think of elephants right away. They have the longest noses of all, and their trunks are excellent tools. An elephant can suck up water with its trunk like a straw and shoot it into its mouth. An elephant doesn't see well, but it has a great sense of smell. When it smells a lion or another predator creeping near, it uses its trunk to trumpet warnings to the rest of the herd. An elephant's trunk also serves as its hand. It can pick up small bits of food or gently soothe the young with a pleasant massage.

A tapir's nose is nothing like an elephant's, but it certainly does dangle a bit. A tapir has an excellent sense of smell. It can sniff its way through the densest, darkest forest. When a tapir smells tasty leaves on an upper branch, it stretches up its trunk, grasps the branch, and pulls it down to its mouth so it can gobble the leaves.

Other mammals with extra-long noses also have a strong sense of smell. An elephant shrew, for instance, uses its long, pointed nose to probe for insects hidden in the grass. It also leaves scents with its scent glands so other elephant shrews will know it is there. An anteater has a really long snout. It follows its nose to an ant nest and uses its long sticky tongue to lap up the ants hiding inside.

A tapir's long snout helps it sniff its way through dense brush.

Bandicoots and echidnas also have long noses that they use to root out insects and earthworms hidden from view.

Many mammals have noses that are specially adapted to the places they live. When a beaver or an otter dives underwater, it closes off its nostrils with special muscles. A manatee, which spends all its time in the water, has nostrils on the top of its nose. When it comes up to breathe, only its nostrils stick out. When it dives, special valves close off the nostrils. Seals and platypuses also close off their nostrils underwater. The platypus uses its leathery snout to probe for worms and insects in the muddy bottom of its pond.

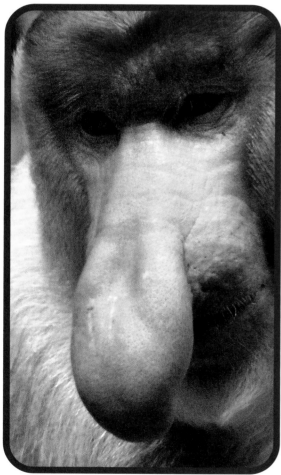

A male proboscis monkey's big nose helps it attract females.

Some mammals have uniquely shaped snouts. Look at the bulging nose of a male proboscis monkey. It certainly stands out on his face, but it is a big help to the monkey. His big nose acts as a loudspeaker when he calls out to the other members of the group, especially any females that might be interested in mating. The females are also drawn to the large, dangling snout.

A star-nosed mole also has a memorable nose. It has twenty-two pink finger-like feelers on its snout that look like a star. These feelers are very sensitive to touch. The nearly blind mole can easily sense worms and other tasty treats underground using the many feelers on its nose.

A star-nosed mole uses its twenty-two pink feelers to help make up for the fact that it is nearly blind.

Some mammals have other parts included on their snouts. Rhinoceroses, for instance, have one or two spear-like horns on their nose. These spears are not made of bone, but of *keratin*, the same stuff hair is made of. A rhinoceros's horn, like hair, keeps growing all its life. The longest rhino horn ever found was 5 feet (152 centimeters). If a rhino's horn breaks off, it will soon grow back. Females use their nose horns to protect their young, butting and stabbing at attackers.

A male narwhal is another mammal with a spear on its nose. The long spear is actually a tooth, which sticks through the narwhal's left upper lip. Narwhals do not use their spears for fighting, though, but to attract a female. Females are drawn to a male's long nose growth.

Droopy noses, button noses, long noses—mammal noses come in all shapes and sizes. They help their owners find food, recognize mates, and stay safe. Mammal noses work in many different ways.

GLOSSARY

abdomen—The third and last part of an insect's body.

cloaca—An opening under the tail of reptiles, amphibians, and birds that gets rid of wastes.

diaphragm—A muscle under a mammal's lungs that pushes air in and out.

echolocation—Finding the way or detecting nearby objects by sending out sound signals and then listening for the echo.

keratin—The material a rhinoceros's horn is made of.

larva—The young of many animals.

naiad—The young of some aquatic insects.

nasal cavity—A space inside the skull leading to the nose.

nasolabial groove—One of two grooves on a lungless salamander's snout that help it smell.

odor particle—A tiny bit floating in the air from which the nose detects an odor.

olfactory bulb—A structure above the nasal cavity containing nerve cells that detect odors.

olfactory nerve—A nerve leading from the olfactory bulb to the brain.

ovipositor—A tube on the end of a female insect's tail used for laying eggs.

pharynx—An area in the throat between the mouth cavity and the esophagus.

pheromone—A chemical signal many animals produce that can be detected by other animals of the same species.

plankton—Tiny animal and plant life floating in the water.

smell receptor—One of several organs on an insect's body that detect odors.

spiracle—An opening in an insect's side that allows air to flow through.

swim bladder—An air-filled structure inside a fish that allows it to rise or sink in the water.

trachea—A tube that carries air into an animal's body.

turbinate—One of several shelf-like bones in a mammal's nose covered by a membrane that creates mucus.

vomeronasal organ—An organ at the base of some animals' nasal cavities that allows them to smell and taste.

FIND OUT MORE

BOOKS

Barre, Michel. *Animal Senses*. Milwaukee, WI: Gareth Stevens, 1998.

Cerfolli, Fulvio. *Adapting to the Environment*. Austin, TX: Raintree Steck-Vaughn, 1999.

Hickman, Pamela, and Pat Stephens. *Animal Senses: How Animals See, Hear, Taste, Smell, and Feel*. Buffalo, NY: Kids Can Press, 1998.

Parker, Steve. *Adaptation*. Chicago, IL: Heinemann Library, 2001.

Santa Fe Writers Group. *Bizarre and Beautiful Noses*. Santa Fe: NM: John Muir, 1993.

Savage, Stephen. *Noses*. Toronto, Ontario: Thomson Learning, 1995.

Viegas, Jennifer. *The Mouth and Nose: Learning How We Taste and Smell*. New York: Rosen, 2002.

ORGANIZATIONS AND WEB SITES

The Animal Diversity Web
http://animaldiversity.ummz.umich.edu
This site contains information about individual species in several different classes of animals, particularly mammals.

Audubon Society
http://www.audubon.org
This organization is an amazing source of information for people interested in birds and bird-watching.

Cyber School—Marine Life
http://ourworld.compuserve.com/Homepages/jaap/Mnlinks.htm
This site provides information on many fishes and other marine life.

Insect Inspecta World
http://www.insecta-inspecta.com
This site has all kinds of information about insects.

Neuroscience for Kids—Amazing Animal Senses
http://faculty.washington.edu/chudler/amaze.html
At this site you can learn a lot of amazing facts about animal senses.

INDEX

Page numbers for illustrations are in **boldface**.

air, 12, 15, 17, 25, 26, 28, 29, 30, 33, 34, 36, 39
alligator, 29, **29**
amphibians, 25-28
ants, 9, 10, **10**

bills, 33, 35, 36
birds, 33-37
blood vessels, 5, 15, 16, 17, 26, 28, 41
blowhole, 39
brain, 5, 17, 19, 27, 40
breathing, 5, 7, 11, 15, 16, 25, 29, 33, 34, 39, 40, 44

chest, 5, 39

diaphragm, 39
dogs, 5, **40**, 41

eggs, 9, 19
elephant, **4**, 5, 42, 43

fish, 15-23
food, 9, 10, 19, 27, 30, 35, 36, 42, 43

frogs, **24**, 25

gills, 13, 15, 16, 17, 25, 28

hair, 5, 9, 17, 45

insects, 5, 9-13, 36, 40, 41, 43

lungs, 5, 16, 17, 25, 26, 28, 29, 33, 34, 39

mammals, 39-45
mating, 9, 18, 23, 27, 31, 35, 37, 42, 44
mouth, 15, 16, 17, 25, 26, 28, 30, 42, 43

nasal cavity, 5, 26, 41
nerve cells, 5, 6, 41
nostrils, 5, 7, 15, 17, 19, 21, 25, 27, 28, 29, 31, 33, 35, 36, 39, 41, 42, 44

odor particles, 5
olfactory bulb, 5, 40, 41
olfactory nerve, 6

oxygen, 5, 12, 13, 15, 16, 17, 25, 26, 28, 29, 33, 34, 39

pheromones, 10-11, 18
prey, 18, 19, 21, 22, 23, 29, 31, 36, 40

reptiles, 25, 28-31

salamanders, 25, 26-27, **27**
skin, 16, 18, 22, 25, 26
smell, 5, 6, 7, 9, 17, 19, 21, 26, 27, 28, 29, 30, 34-35, 36, 40, 41, 42, 43
snakes, 28, 30-31, **31**
spiracles, 11, **11**
swim bladder, 15

tail, 12, 13, 16, 29
taste buds, 7, 19
tongue, 7, 19, 30, 43, 44
trachea, 11, 34

water, 11, 12, 13, 15, 16, 17, 18, 25, 26, 28, 29, 40, 42, 44
windpipe, 5

ABOUT THE AUTHOR

Sara Swan Miller has enjoyed working with children all her life, first as a Montessori nursery school teacher and later as an outdoor environmental educator at the Mohonk Preserve in New Paltz, New York. As director of the school program, she has taught hundreds of children the importance of appreciating the natural world.

She has written more than fifty books, including *Three Stories You Can Read to Your Dog; Three Stories You Can Read to Your Cat; Three More Stories You Can Read to Your Dog; Three More Stories You Can Read to Your Cat; Three Stories You Can Read to Your Teddy Bear; Will You Sting Me? Will You Bite? The Truth About Some Scary-Looking Insects;* and *What's in the Woods? An Outdoor Activity Book.* She has also written many nonfiction books for children.